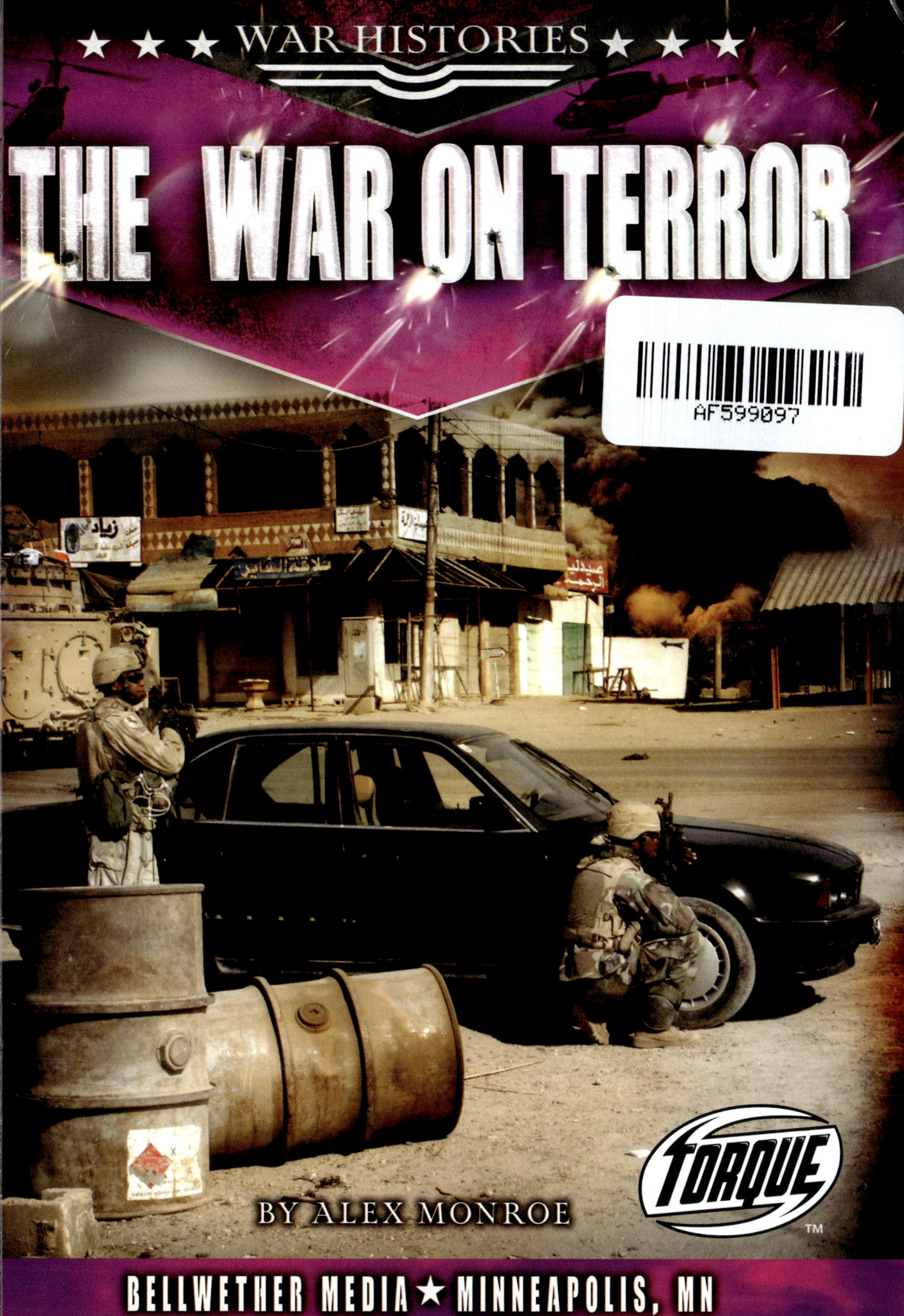
WAR HISTORIES
THE WAR ON TERROR
AF599097
BY ALEX MONROE
TORQUE
BELLWETHER MEDIA ★ MINNEAPOLIS, MN

Torque brims with excitement perfect for thrill-seekers of all kinds. Discover daring survival skills, explore uncharted worlds, and marvel at mighty engines and extreme sports. In *Torque* books, anything can happen. Are you ready?

This edition first published in 2025 by Bellwether Media, Inc.

Library of Congress Cataloging-in-Publication Data

LC record for The War on Terror available at: https://lccn.loc.gov/2024035376

Editor: Rebecca Sabelko Designer: Josh Brink

Printed in the United States of America, North Mankato, MN.

TABLE OF CONTENTS

WHAT WAS THE WAR ON TERROR?

The War on Terror took place from 2001 to 2021. The United States and other nations fought **Islamist extremists**. They fought al-Qaeda, a **terrorist** group. They also fought the Taliban. This dangerous group has held control in Afghanistan.

Fighting mostly took place in the **Middle East**. It was the longest war in U.S. history.

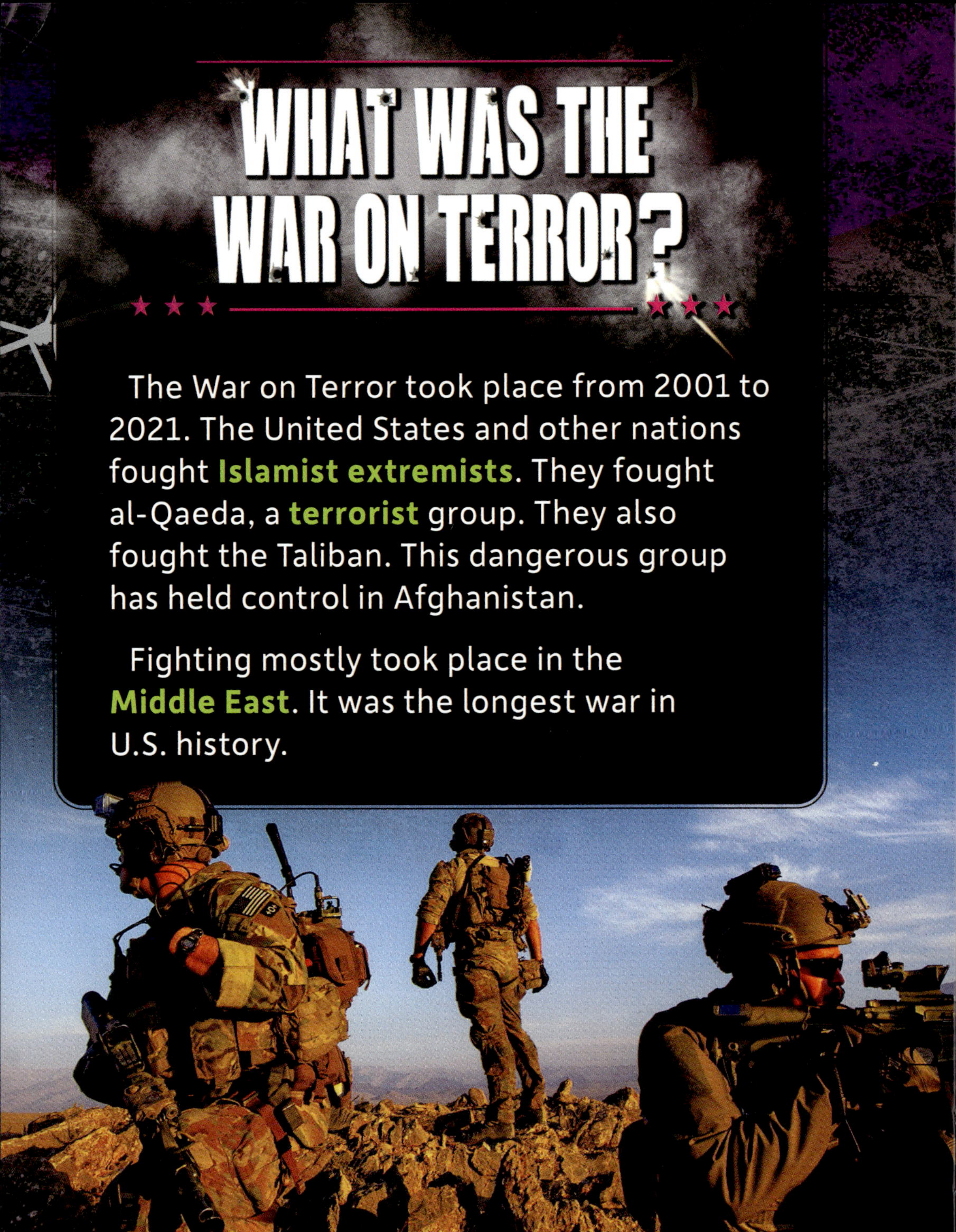

★ WAR ON TERROR MAP ★

WARS WITHIN A WAR

The War in Afghanistan and the Iraq War were parts of the War on Terror.

A GROWING THREAT

Osama bin Laden created al-Qaeda in 1988. He was an Islamist extremist. The U.S. stayed in the Middle East after the **Gulf War** in 1991. Bin Laden wanted the U.S. out.

ATTACK ON THE U.S. EMBASSY IN KENYA

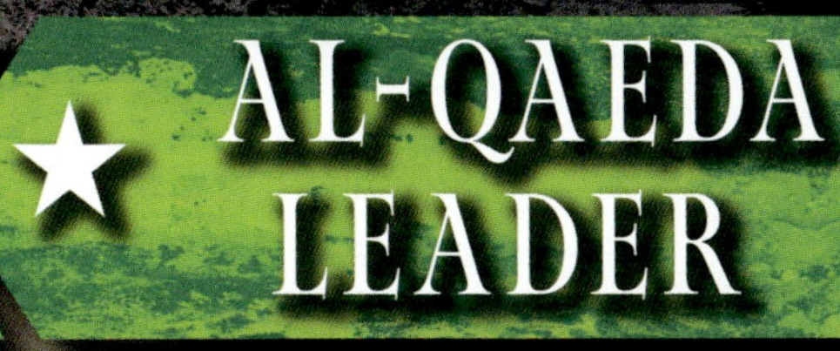

AL-QAEDA LEADER

NAME
Osama bin Laden

NATIONALITY
Saudi Arabian

POSITION
al-Qaeda Leader (1988 to 2011)

IMPORTANT ACTIONS

- 1988: Formed al-Qaeda
- 1990s: Led attacks against the U.S.
- 2001: Planned 9/11

Al-Qaeda attacked the U.S. It bombed the World Trade Center in New York in 1993. In 1998, it attacked U.S. **embassies** in East Africa. It bombed the USS *Cole* in 2000.

UNDER ATTACK

The War on Terror began on September 11, 2001, or 9/11. Al-Qaeda crashed planes into the World Trade Center and the **Pentagon**. Another plane crashed in Pennsylvania. It was the biggest attack on U.S. soil.

9/11 WORLD TRADE CENTER ATTACK

★ 9/11 PLANE CRASHES ★

The U.S. learned bin Laden was in Afghanistan. But the Taliban would not help the U.S. catch him. U.S. President George W. Bush ordered the **War in Afghanistan** on October 7.

The U.S. and other nations entered eastern Afghanistan in December 2001. Leaders believed bin Laden was hiding there. The U.S. did not find him. But they took the Taliban out of power. The war continued.

★ U.S. LEADER ★

NAME
George W. Bush

NATIONALITY
American

POSITION
U.S. President (2001 to 2009)

IMPORTANT ACTIONS

- 2001: Began the War in Afghanistan
- 2002: Helped make the Department of Homeland Security
- 2003: Began the Iraq War

President Bush stated that he wanted to rebuild Afghanistan's government in April 2002. He felt it would help bring peace. But efforts were unsuccessful by the end of the war.

The **Iraq War** began in March 2003. The U.S. said Iraqi leader Saddam Hussein had deadly weapons. Later, Hussein was caught. But war did not end in Iraq.

The U.S. used **drones** during many conflicts. They were used to track enemies. They also fired **missiles** at enemies. Pilots flew drones from far away. This kept pilots safe.

MQ-1 PREDATOR DRONE

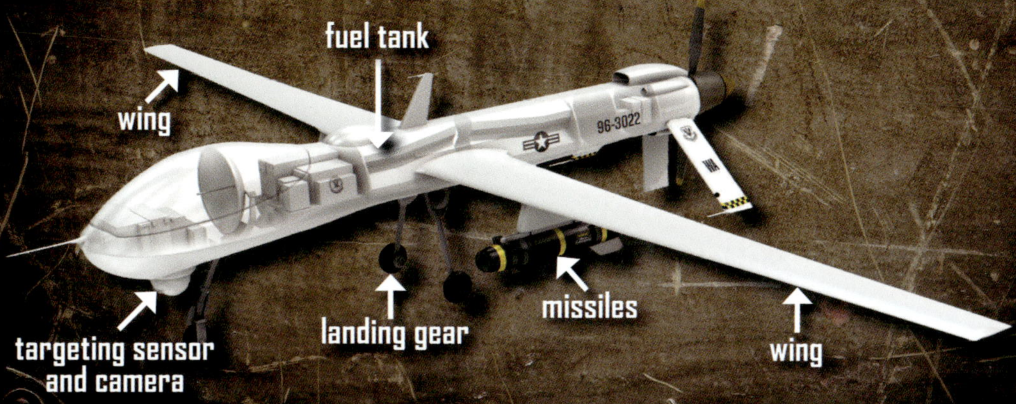

WORLDWIDE ATTACKS

Extremists made terrorist attacks worldwide during the war. They made surprise attacks. They carried out quick strikes against enemies.

THE WAR CARRIES ON

At first, many people supported the War on Terror. In 2004, people learned Iraq did not have deadly weapons. They later learned U.S. drone strikes hurt many **civilians**. People felt misled. They lost trust in U.S. leaders. They spoke out against the war.

THE WAR AT HOME

Security in the U.S. grew during the War on Terror. Airports limited what people could bring on planes. New laws let the U.S. government get personal information on civilians. This included records of phone calls.

Some people liked the changes. They felt safer. Others did not. They felt they lost their rights. Many of these changes unfairly targeted Muslims.

AIRPORT SECURITY

Some people treated **Muslims** harshly after 9/11. They wrongly thought Muslims held the same beliefs as extremists.

TROOPS RETURNING TO THE U.S. FROM IRAQ

U.S. and Iraqi leaders met in 2008. They agreed U.S. troops would leave Iraq in 2011. The last U.S. troops left Iraq in December 2011. The Iraq War was over.

U.S. leaders tried to end the War in Afghanistan in the 2010s. There were peace talks. But they did not work.

BIN LADEN'S END

Bin Laden died in May 2011. He was taken down by U.S. troops.

U.S. PRESIDENT BARACK OBAMA MEETING WITH THE AFGHAN PRESIDENT IN 2013

LEAVING THE WAR

U.S. President Joe Biden had troops start leaving Afghanistan in 2021. The Taliban quickly took over the Afghan government. Afghan civilians feared for their safety. Many fled the country.

U.S. troops kept leaving Afghanistan. The last U.S. troops left on August 30. The War in Afghanistan was over. The War on Terror was over, too.

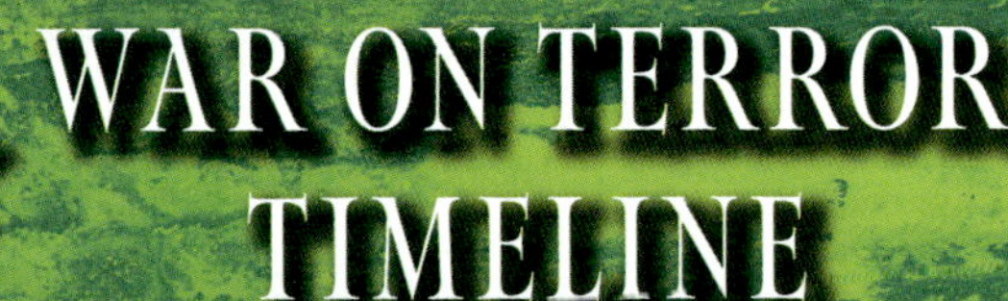

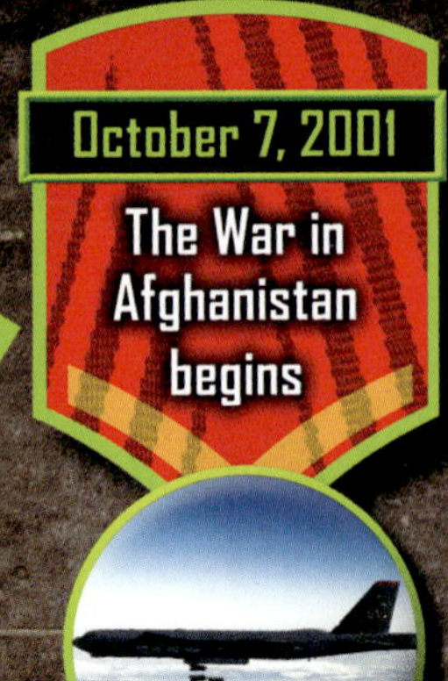

U.S. TROOPS LEAVING AFGHANISTAN

December 18, 2011
The Iraq War ends

August 15, 2021
The Taliban retakes control of Afghanistan

August 30, 2021
The last U.S. troops leave Afghanistan

The War on Terror led to more defense in the U.S. The Department of Homeland Security began in 2003. It was made to keep the U.S. safe. It still exists today.

The war harmed many people. Thousands of civilians died. Many more lost their homes. The War on Terror will affect people for years to come.

U.S. PRESIDENT JOE BIDEN AT AN EVENT FOR THE DEPARTMENT OF HOMELAND SECURITY

★ BY THE NUMBERS ★

10,000 people = [icon]

OVERALL COST FOR THE U.S.

- around $11.6 trillion (in 2024 dollars)

ESTIMATED NUMBER OF DEATHS

- U.S.: around 7,000 troops
- Civilians: more than 432,000 people
- Opponents: more than 295,000 fighters

TOTAL U.S. MILITARY PERSONNEL DEPLOYED

- around 3 million

GLOSSARY

civilians—people who do not belong to a nation's armed forces

drones—remote-controlled devices that use cameras to get around

embassies—official offices for people serving their government in a foreign country

Gulf War—a conflict from 1990 to 1991 involving many countries after Iraq invaded Kuwait

Iraq War—a U.S.-led war fought between Iraq and many other countries that lasted from 2003 to 2011

Islamist extremists—people who believe governments should follow the Islamic laws of their choosing, but whose beliefs go against the social and moral beliefs of most people; Muslims do not share the same beliefs as Islamist extremists.

Middle East—a region of southwestern Asia and northern Africa; this region includes Egypt, Iran, Iraq, Israel, Saudi Arabia, Syria, and other nearby countries.

missiles—weapons that travel in the air and explode when they hit a target

Muslims—people who practice the Islamic faith; Islam is a religion based on belief in Allah as the only God and in the Prophet Muhammad as God's follower.

Pentagon—a building in Arlington, Virginia, that is the main building for the U.S. military

terrorist—related to a group that uses terror as a means of achieving a goal

War in Afghanistan—a U.S.-led war fought between the Taliban and many other countries that lasted from 2001 to 2021

TO LEARN MORE

AT THE LIBRARY

Chandler, Matt. *Drones*. Minneapolis, Minn.: Bellwether Media, 2022.

Maranville, Amy. *The 9/11 Terrorist Attacks: A Day That Changed America*. North Mankato, Minn.: Capstone Captivate, 2022.

Monroe, Alex. *The Gulf War.* Minneapolis, Minn.: Bellwether Media, 2025.

ON THE WEB

FACTSURFER

Factsurfer.com gives you a safe, fun way to find more information.

1. Go to www.factsurfer.com
2. Enter "War on Terror " into the search box and click 🔍.
3. Select your book cover to see a list of related content.

INDEX

The images in this book are reproduced through the courtesy of: SPC Preston E. Cheeks, USA/ NARA & DVIDS, front cover (hero scene); Defense Visual Information Distribution Service/ NARA & DVIDS, front cover (helicopter right); SSGT Ricky A. Bloom, USAF/ NARA & DVIDS, front cover (helicopter left); GYSGT Keith A. Milks, USMC/ NARA & DVIDS, pp. 2-3, 22-24; Geopix/ Alamy, pp. 4-5; Thomas Coex/ Getty Images, pp. 6-7; Universal Images Group/ Getty Images, p. 7; Laperruque/ Alamy, p. 8; World History Archive/ Alamy, p. 10; Eric Draper/ Wiki Commons, pp. 11, 21 (George W. Bush); Robert Nickelsberg/ Getty Images, pp. 12-13; Album/ Alamy, p. 13 (drone feature); Jim Ruymen/ Alamy, pp. 14-15; Douglas McFadd/ Stringer/ Getty Images, p. 15; Association Press/ AP Newsroom, pp. 16, 17; rds323/ Wiki Commons, p. 18 (September 11, 2001); USAF/ Getty Images, p. 18 (October 7, 2001); Aamir Qureshi/ Getty Images, pp. 18-19; Pool Getty/ AP Newsroom, p. 19 (December 18, 2011); World Politics Archive/ Alamy, pp. 20-21; Pete Souza/ Wiki Commons, p. 21 (Barack Obama); Presidency of Ukraine/ Wiki Commons, p. 21 (Donald Trump); David Lienemann/ Wiki Commons, p. 21 (Joe Biden).